Lancaster Castle

Favourite Lancashire Recipes

compiled by
Dorothy Baldock

with illustrations
by Albert Woods

SALMON

INDEX

Cover pictures: *front*, The Market Cross, Inglewhite
back, North-east Gateway, Whalley Abbey

Printed and Published by J. Salmon Ltd., Sevenoaks, England ©

Lancashire Hot Pot

2 lb. middle end of neck of lamb, divided into 8 cutlets
1 oz. lard or dripping
4 onions, peeled and sliced
4 carrots, peeled and sliced or
½ lb. mushrooms, wiped and quartered
2 lb. potatoes, peeled and thinly sliced
Salt and black pepper
2 pints lamb stock
Chopped fresh parsley to garnish

Set oven to 325°F or Mark 3. Trim any excess fat from the cutlets. Heat the lard or dripping in a frying pan and lightly brown the cutlets on both sides. In a large ovenproof casserole, layer up the cutlets, onions, carrots and potatoes, seasoning each layer successively, finishing with a neat 'thatch' of potatoes. Pour in the stock. Sprinkle a little salt over the potato 'thatch' and brush with melted lard or dripping. Cover and cook for 1½ to 2 hours. Remove from the oven and brush the potatoes with a little more melted lard or dripping and cook, uncovered, for a further 20 to 30 minutes until the potatoes are golden brown and crisp. Serve garnished with parsley and accompanied by pickled red cabbage or plain boiled red cabbage, if preferred. Serves 4.

The name comes from the straight-sided earthenware dish in which the dish was traditionally cooked. There are many variations of Hot Pot recipes – one of them contained oysters – but all Hot Pots are 'thatched' with a layer of sliced potato.

Salmesbury in Lower Ribblesdale

Harcake or Soul-mass Cake

2 oz. butter, softened
1 lb. fine oatmeal
12 fl oz. golden syrup
½ oz. ground ginger
1 egg, beaten
A little brown ale

Set oven to 350°F or Mark 4. Grease and base-line a deep 10 x 8 inch baking tin. Rub the butter into the oatmeal, then add the syrup and ginger and combine well. Add the egg and sufficient ale to make a thick, smooth batter. Pour into the prepared tin and cook for 1 to 1½ hours, until firm yet springy, covering the top with foil if it seems to be browning too quickly. Cool in the tin for 5 minutes, then turn out on to a wire rack. When completely cold, cut into squares and store in an air-tight tin for 1 week before eating.

A gingercake traditionally eaten at Hallowe'en, when the departed are remembered.

Blackburn Fig Pie

8 oz. dried figs
8 oz. shortcrust pastry
1 level tablespoon cornflour
2 tablespoons soft brown sugar
1 teaspoon mixed spice
1 oz. raisins
Milk or beaten egg to glaze

Sometimes called Fag Pie, this was a Mothering Sunday dish – so popular that Mothering Sunday was often referred to as Fig or Fag Sunday.

Soak figs overnight in cold water to which a little lemon juice has been added. Next morning, drain figs well, reserving the liquid, and chop roughly. Set oven to 400°F or Mark 6. Roll out pastry on a lightly floured surface and use to line a lightly greased 8 inch pie plate. Cover with foil and bake blind for 15 to 20 minutes. Blend cornflour to a smooth paste with a little of the fig liquid. Put remainder of liquid into a saucepan and add sugar, spice and raisins. Heat through, then stir in the cornflour and add the chopped figs. Bring to the boil, stirring, then simmer to thicken and reduce the liquid. Remove pastry case from oven and reduce heat to 375°F or Mark 5. Fill with the fig mixture and brush pastry edges with milk or beaten egg to glaze. Bake for 15 to 20 minutes, until pastry is golden. Serve with custard or cream. Serves 4 to 6.

Hindle Wakes Chicken

One 4 to 4½ lb. oven-ready chicken
1 medium onion, peeled and sliced
Salt and black pepper
Cold water
¼ pint white wine vinegar
1 tablespoon brown sugar
Lemon slices and parsley sprigs to garnish

STUFFING:
4 oz. breadcrumbs
8 oz. prunes, stoned and chopped
Salt and black pepper
Pinch of cinnamon
Pinch of mace
1 tablespoon chopped fresh parsley, sage and thyme, mixed
1 small shallot peeled and finely chopped
1 tablespoon melted butter
1 teaspoon grated lemon rind
2 tablespoons lemon juice

Mix together stuffing ingredients and stuff chicken, sewing up with thread. Place chicken in large saucepan with onion and seasoning and just cover with cold water. Add vinegar and sugar and bring to boil, cover and simmer very gently for 2½ to 3 hours. Allow chicken to cool in liquid, then skim to remove surface fat. Lift out chicken and drain well, reserving liquid. Remove thread and skin and place chicken on large dish to cool. Sauce: Melt 1 oz. butter in saucepan, stir in ½ oz. of flour and cook for 1 minute. Strain in the chicken liquid, a little at a time, stirring until creamy and smooth. Add 1 teaspoon lemon juice and grated rind of 1 lemon and cook for 1 to 2 minutes, stirring. Allow to cool, covering with butter paper to prevent a skin forming, then pour over chicken. Serve cold, garnished with lemon slices and parsley and with 12–18 stewed prunes.

Savoury Pudding

A full ½ pint milk
2 oz. fine oatmeal
2 oz. fresh breadcrumbs
1 egg
1½ oz. flour
2 oz. finely chopped suet
1 dessertspoon chopped fresh thyme, parsley and sage, mixed
Salt and black pepper
1 onion, peeled and very finely chopped
A 'walnut' of butter

Warm the milk in a pan and mix in the oatmeal and breadcrumbs. Allow to stand for 30 minutes, then beat in the egg. Set oven to 375°F or Mark 5. In a bowl, mix together the flour, suet, herbs and seasoning, then stir in the onion and combine with the oatmeal mixture. Beat well, adding a little extra milk if necessary. Turn into a well-greased pie dish and smooth the top. Dot with the butter and cook for 45 minutes; cover the top with kitchen foil if the pudding appears to be browning too quickly. Serve hot, cut into wedges, as an accompaniment to roast pork or roast goose. Serves 4.

A nineteenth century farmhouse dish which sometimes included prunes in the ingredients.

Hindle Wakes Chicken

One 4 to 4½ lb. oven-ready chicken
1 medium onion, peeled and sliced
Salt and black pepper
Cold water
¼ pint white wine vinegar
1 tablespoon brown sugar
Lemon slices and parsley sprigs to garnish
STUFFING:
4 oz. breadcrumbs
8 oz. prunes, stoned and chopped
Salt and black pepper
Pinch of cinnamon
Pinch of mace
1 tablespoon chopped fresh parsley, sage and thyme, mixed
1 small shallot peeled and finely chopped
1 tablespoon melted butter
1 teaspoon grated lemon rind
2 tablespoons lemon juice

Mix together stuffing ingredients and stuff chicken, sewing up with thread. Place chicken in large saucepan with onion and seasoning and just cover with cold water. Add vinegar and sugar and bring to boil, cover and simmer very gently for 2½ to 3 hours. Allow chicken to cool in liquid, then skim to remove surface fat. Lift out chicken and drain well, reserving liquid. Remove thread and skin and place chicken on large dish to cool. Sauce: Melt 1 oz. butter in saucepan, stir in ½ oz. of flour and cook for 1 minute. Strain in the chicken liquid, a little at a time, stirring until creamy and smooth. Add 1 teaspoon lemon juice and grated rind of 1 lemon and cook for 1 to 2 minutes, stirring. Allow to cool, covering with butter paper to prevent a skin forming, then pour over chicken. Serve cold, garnished with lemon slices and parsley and with 12–18 stewed prunes.

Lancashire Foots

1 lb. shortcrust pastry
4 oz. Lancashire cheese, cubed
4 oz. cooked bacon or ham, chopped
1 small onion, peeled and chopped
Salt and black pepper
A little dry English mustard
Milk or beaten egg to glaze

Popular with miners, these pasties, sometimes known as Collier's Foots, can have a variety of savoury fillings. Eliptical in shape – hence the name – they are always made in pairs and always called 'foots' never 'feet'.

Set oven to 375°F or Mark 5. Roll out the pastry on a lightly floured surface to form an oval. Cut in half lengthwise and separate the two pieces. Place a rolling pin across the middle of each piece and roll away from you. The pastry nearest you remains un-rolled and thicker and is the 'heel', while the rolled piece is the 'sole'. Combine together the cheese, bacon or ham, onion and seasoning. Divide this mixture into two halves and pile up in the centre of each heel. Brush the edges of the 'foots' with milk, then turn the 'soles' over to enclose the filling, sealing the edges well. Brush with milk or beaten egg to glaze and place on a greased baking sheet. Cook for 25 to 30 minutes, or until the 'foots' are golden brown. Serve warm or cold.

The Market Square, Garstang

Savoury Pudding

A full ½ pint milk
2 oz. fine oatmeal
2 oz. fresh breadcrumbs
1 egg
1½ oz. flour
2 oz. finely chopped suet
1 dessertspoon chopped fresh thyme, parsley and sage, mixed
Salt and black pepper
1 onion, peeled and very finely chopped
A 'walnut' of butter

Warm the milk in a pan and mix in the oatmeal and breadcrumbs. Allow to stand for 30 minutes, then beat in the egg. Set oven to 375°F or Mark 5. In a bowl, mix together the flour, suet, herbs and seasoning, then stir in the onion and combine with the oatmeal mixture. Beat well, adding a little extra milk if necessary. Turn into a well-greased pie dish and smooth the top. Dot with the butter and cook for 45 minutes; cover the top with kitchen foil if the pudding appears to be browning too quickly. Serve hot, cut into wedges, as an accompaniment to roast pork or roast goose. Serves 4.

A nineteenth century farmhouse dish which sometimes included prunes in the ingredients.

Eccles Cakes

8 oz. puff pastry
2 oz. butter, melted
6 oz. currants
1 teaspoon mixed spice
1 oz. soft brown sugar
Milk or a little lightly beaten egg white
A little granulated sugar

Chorley Cakes, from the neighbouring town of Chorley, are very similar, except that they contain mixed peel and have 4 'slashes'. Lancashire cakes are made in the same way, but with yeast dough instead of puff pastry. They are pricked, not 'slashed' before baking, and when cooked resemble fruit-filled buns.

Set oven to 450°F or Mark 8. Roll out the pastry thinly on a lightly floured surface and cut into 4-inch rounds. Mix together the butter, currants, spice and sugar and place generous spoonfuls in the centre of each round. Dampen the edge of the pastry, draw up into the centre, like a parcel to enclose the filling and seal well. Turn over and flatten very lightly with a rolling pin. With a knife, make 3 'slashes' across the top of each cake, brush with milk or egg white and sprinkle with sugar. Place on a greased baking sheet and bake for 15 minutes or until golden. Serve warm. Makes about 8.

These little cakes are believed to date back to medieval days, and they were originally served at religious festivals – the three 'slashes' being said to represent the Holy Trinity.

Rivington Pike near Bolton

Tripe and Onions

1 lb. dressed tripe, washed
3 onions, peeled and sliced
1½ pint milk
2 oz. butter
2 oz. flour
Salt and black pepper
Pinch of nutmeg
Chopped fresh parsley to garnish

Put the tripe in a saucepan, cover with cold water and bring to the boil. Drain and rinse under cold, running water, then cut into 1 to 2 inch pieces. Put the tripe, onions and milk into a saucepan, bring to the boil, then cover and simmer for 1½ to 2 hours, or until the tripe is tender. Strain off the milk and reserve. Melt the butter in a saucepan, then stir in the flour and cook gently for 1 minute. Gradually add the milk and bring to the boil, stirring continuously until a creamy sauce is obtained. Season and add the nutmeg, tripe and onions and heat through thoroughly. Transfer to a heated serving dish and serve at once, garnished with parsley. Serves 4. If desired, the tripe and onions can be transferred to a flameproof dish, sprinkled with grated Lancashire cheese and browned lightly under the grill before serving.

Poor Man's Cake

¾ lb. self-raising flour
½ teaspoon baking powder
1 oz. butter
6 oz. soft brown sugar
Milk
1 egg, beaten

Set oven to 350°F or Mark 4. In a bowl, sift the flour and baking powder together, then rub in the butter. Stir in the sugar, then add sufficient milk to form a stiff dough. On a lightly floured surface, form into a teacake shape. Place on a well-greased baking sheet and brush liberally with beaten egg to glaze. Bake for 30 to 40 minutes until golden brown. Serve sliced, with or without butter.

Although not traditional, ½ teaspoon of mixed spice and 1 to 1½ oz. dried fruit can be added to the mixture, with the sugar.

Morecambe Bay Potted Shrimps

1 lb. shelled shrimps or prawns
6 oz. butter
1 to 2 teaspoons anchovy essence
½ teaspoon mace
Pinch of cayenne pepper
Salt

Set oven to 325°F or Mark 3. Cut the shrimps or prawns in half. In a saucepan melt 4 oz. of the butter with the anchovy essence, spices and salt. Put the shrimps or prawns in an oven-proof dish, pour the butter mixture over, cover and cook in the oven for 15 to 20 minutes. Drain the shrimps or prawns well, reserving the butter mixture and pack into small jars or moulds. Strain the reserved butter mixture and pour over the shrimps or prawns, dividing it evenly. Leave to set. Melt the remaining 2 oz. butter and pour onto the jars or moulds to seal the mixture. Place in the refrigerator overnight before serving. Serve with brown bread or fingers of toast. Serves 4 to 6.

Morecambe Bay Shrimps – small and brown – are considered to be among the finest in the country and have been popular since the 18th century.

Cow Heel and Beef Tart

½ a cow heel, 'dressed' by the butcher
½ lb. shin of beef
6 cloves
1 medium onion, peeled
1 pint beef stock
Salt and black pepper
1 lb. shortcrust pastry
Beaten egg to glaze

Put the cow heel and the beef into a saucepan. Push the cloves into the onion and add to the pan with the stock and seasoning. Bring to the boil, cover and simmer for 2½ to 3 hours. Lift out the cow heel, beef and onion, set aside and allow to cool a little. Strip the meat from the cow heel and cut up all the meat into small pieces. Remove the cloves and chop the onion finely. Strain the stock and reserve. Set oven to 375°F or Mark 5. Roll out the pastry on a lightly floured surface and use half to line a greased 8-inch flan ring, set on a baking sheet. Add the meat and onion and moisten with a very little of the stock. Cover with the remaining pastry; seal and trim the edges. Make a steam hole. Brush with beaten egg and bake for 45 to 50 minutes or until the pastry is golden. Remove the flan ring. Serve the 'tart' with mashed potatoes, carrots and butter beans. Serves 4 to 6.

Parson Lane and the Castle, Clitheroe

Damson Fool

1½ lb. damsons, washed
6 oz. sugar, or more if the damsons are very tart
1 teaspoon lemon juice (optional)
½ pint double cream
2 egg whites

Put the damsons in a saucepan with the sugar and lemon juice (if desired) and sufficient water to cover. Bring to the boil, then simmer, very gently until the fruit is soft. Cool and remove the stones, then sieve or liquidise the mixture and turn the purée into a large bowl. Whip the cream until it will hold its shape, then whisk the egg whites until they stand up in peaks. Add the cream and the egg white to the fruit purée and combine gently, ensuring that the colour is even. Turn into a glass bowl and serve with whipped cream, sponge fingers or cat's tongue biscuits. Serves 4 to 6.

In Lancashire, damsons, despite their tartness, are often served raw as a 'relish' with Lancashire cheese.

Manchester Pudding

½ pint milk
1 oz. butter
½ oz. caster sugar
3 oz. fresh white breadcrumbs
2 eggs, separated
Grated rind of ½ a lemon
1 tablespoon sherry or brandy
4 heaped tablespoons apricot jam
1 oz. caster sugar

In some versions of Manchester Pudding, the jam is spread direct on to the uncooked breadcrumb mixture, topped with the meringue and the whole pudding cooked together.

Put the milk, butter and ½ oz. sugar into a saucepan and bring to the boil, stirring. Pour on to the breadcrumbs in a bowl and allow to stand for 10 to 15 minutes. Set oven to 350°F or Mark 4. Beat the egg yolks lightly and stir into the mixture with the lemon rind and sherry or brandy. Butter a 1 to 1½ pint pie dish and spread 2 tablespoons of apricot jam over the base. Top with the breadcrumb mixture. Place the pie dish in a roasting tin half-filled with water, and cook in the oven for 20 minutes, until lightly set. Warm the remaining apricot jam and spread it over the pudding. Whisk the egg whites with the 1 oz. sugar until they stand up in stiff peaks and pipe or spoon on to the jam. Return to the oven for a further 20 minutes until the meringue is crisp and lightly browned. Serve cold, accompanied by single cream. Serves 4.

Mawdesley in the Hundred of Leyland

Goosnargh Cakes

8 oz. flour
Pinch of salt
6 oz. butter
½ teaspoon caraway seeds
½ teaspoon ground coriander
1 oz. caster sugar
A little extra sugar

Not really cakes at all, but a spicy shortbread. The traditional way to make Goosnargh Cakes was to form the dough into a neat square and place on a baking sheet. When cooked, it was cut into squares while still warm.

In a bowl, sift the flour and salt together, then rub in the butter until the mixture resembles fine breadcrumbs and work together until a smooth dough is formed. Turn out on to a lightly floured surface and roll out to ¼ inch in thickness, then cut into 2-inch rounds. Place on a large, well-greased baking sheet. Mix together the spices and sugar and sprinkle over the cakes. Leave in a cool place overnight. Set oven to 300°F or Mark 2 and bake the cakes for 40 to 50 minutes until firm, but still quite pale in colour. Place on a wire rack and sprinkle over the extra sugar while still warm. Makes about 16.

Potato Pie

¾ lb. stewing steak, cut into cubes
Seasoned flour
Cooking oil or dripping
1 onion, peeled and sliced
2 carrots, peeled and sliced (optional)
½ to ¾ pint beef stock
1 dessertspoon chopped fresh parsley
Salt and black pepper
1 lb. potatoes, peeled, parboiled and sliced
8 oz. shortcrust pastry
Milk or beaten egg to glaze

Dust the steak with the seasoned flour. Heat the oil or dripping in a saucepan and fry the steak and onion until very lightly browned. Add the carrot (if desired) stock, parsley and seasoning, bring to the boil, cover and simmer for 45 to 60 minutes or until the meat is tender. Transfer to a 2 pint pie dish and cover with the sliced potatoes. Set oven to 375°F or Mark 5. Roll out the pastry on a lightly floured surface and use to cover the pie, sealing the edges and trimming neatly; use the trimmings to decorate. Make a small steam hole. Brush with milk or beaten egg to glaze. Bake for 40 to 50 minutes or until the pastry is golden brown. Serves 4 to 6.

Sometimes the shortcrust pastry is replaced with suet pastry, in which case, bake for 5 to 10 minutes longer.

Blackburn Cracknells

½ lb. flour
2 oz. lard
½ oz. baking powder
¼ pint warm milk

Set oven to 325°F or Mark 3. Sift the flour into a bowl and rub in the lard until the mixture resembles fine breadcrumbs, then add the baking powder and milk. Mix to form a smooth dough, then turn out on a lightly floured surface and knead well. Roll out to ⅛ inch thick and cut into 3 inch rounds. Place on a greased baking sheet and prick with a fork. Cook for 30 minutes or until golden. Cool on a wire rack and store in an airtight tin. Serve with Lancashire cheese. Makes about 30 biscuits.

Lancashire Nuts

4 oz. butter, softened
4 oz. caster sugar
1 egg, beaten
4 oz. flour
½ teaspoon baking powder
4 oz. cornflour

BUTTER-CREAM FILLING:
3 oz. butter, softened
6 oz. icing sugar
A little warm milk

Set oven to 325°F or Mark 3. In a bowl cream the butter and sugar together until fluffy, then beat in the egg, a little at a time. Sift together the flour, baking powder and cornflour and fold into the mixture to form a smooth, stiff dough. On a lightly floured surface, using the hands, roll the mixture into balls each about the size of a walnut and place on a large, well-greased baking sheet. Bake for 25 to 30 minutes until golden. Cool on a wire rack. For the butter-cream, beat the butter until fluffy, then add the icing sugar, beating until smooth and adding a little warm milk, if necessary, to produce a spreading consistency. Use to sandwich the biscuits together. Makes about 16 to 20.

Blackpool from the Sands

Gingerbread Curls

4 oz. flour
1 teaspoon ground ginger
½ teaspoon cinnamon
½ teaspoon mixed spice
3 oz. butter
4 fl. oz. black treacle
4 oz. brown sugar
Grated rind of a lemon

Set oven to 350°F or Mark 4. In a bowl, sift the flour and spices together. Melt the butter in a saucepan and stir in the treacle, sugar and lemon rind. Cook, stirring, until the sugar has completely dissolved. Remove from the heat and stir in the flour mixture, combining well. Drop spoonfuls of this mixture on to a well-greased baking sheet, allowing plenty of room for spread. Bake for 10 to 15 minutes until the edges are crisp. Remove from the baking sheet with a palette knife and, working quickly and carefully whilst hot, roll each one round the well-greased handle of large wooden spoon to form curls. Allow to cool on a wire rack. Serve filled with whipped cream. Makes about 10 to 12.

Similar to Brandy Snaps, but much darker in colour, Gingerbread Curls were originally cooked over an open fire and curled round a poker.

LIVERPOOL SCOUSE

1 to 2 tablespoons cooking oil or dripping
1½ lb. stewing beef, cubed
Salt and black pepper
1 teaspoon chopped fresh thyme
½ to 1 pint beef stock
3 onions, peeled and chopped
4 carrots, peeled and chopped
1 turnip or swede, peeled and chopped
4 medium potatoes, peeled and quartered

Heat the oil or dripping in a large saucepan, add the meat and brown quickly. Add the seasoning, thyme and sufficient stock to cover completely. Bring to the boil, then cover and simmer gently for 1 to 1½ hours. Add the vegetables and continue to simmer for another hour. Serve with pickled red cabbage. Serves 4 to 6.

Based on the 'soup-stew' concocted by sailors whilst at sea, some versions of Scouse contain pork or mutton as well as beef. It is traditionally eaten with a spoon and fork.

Penwortham Church near Preston

Preston Parkin

12 oz. flour
2 teaspoons ground ginger
Pinch of nutmeg
Pinch of mixed spice
2 oz. butter, softened
4 fl. oz. black treacle
½ level teaspoon bicarbonate of soda
3 tablespoons warm milk
1 small egg, beaten

Traditionally enjoyed on 5th November, this 'crunchy' gingerbread, which sometimes contains oatmeal, is very different to the spongier gingerbreads eaten in other parts of the country.

Set oven to 350°F or Mark 4. Grease and line a deep 10 x 8 inch baking tin. In a bowl, sift together the flour and all the spices, then rub in the butter until the mixture resembles fine breadcrumbs. Gently warm the treacle. Add the bicarbonate of soda to the warm milk, then stir into the treacle. Pour the milk/treacle mixture into the flour mixture and combine together. Add the egg, beating the mixture gently, then pour into the prepared tin and bake for about 40 to 50 minutes, or until the parkin is firm yet springy when lightly pressed. Cool in the tin for 5 to 10 minutes, then turn out on to a wire rack. When cold, store in an airtight tin for 2 to 3 days before eating. Serve cut into squares. If preferred half the black treacle can be replaced with golden syrup, though this is not traditional.

Pickled Red Cabbage

One 2 lb. red cabbage, washed, trimmed and finely shredded
Sea salt
1 pint white malt vinegar
1 tablespoon sugar
1 tablespoon pickling spice
A few slices of peeled raw beetroot (optional). This is added to help the cabbage to maintain a good red colour.

Place the cabbage in a bowl and sprinkle with the sea salt. Cover and leave to stand overnight. Next day drain off all the liquid that has accumulated and pack the cabbage into clean, dry, wide-necked jars that have vinegar-proof lids. Place the vinegar, sugar and pickling spice in a saucepan and bring to the boil. Allow to boil for 10 minutes, then cool. Add the beetroot slices (if used) to the jars, then strain in the vinegar, making sure that the cabbage is completely covered. Cover and allow to mature in a cool, dark place for about a month before using. Serve with Lancashire Hot Pot, for which it is a traditional accompaniment, or as a relish with cold meats or Lancashire cheese.

Bury Simnel Cake

3 oz. butter, softened
3 oz. lard
1 lb. self-raising flour
1 teaspoon cinnamon
1 teaspoon nutmeg
10 oz. sugar
1 lb. currants or 8 oz. currants and 8 oz. sultanas
4 oz. candied peel
4 oz. ground almonds
2 large eggs
A little milk

Traditionally made for Mothering Sunday, but resembling a rich curranty bread rather than the more usual marzipan-decorated fruit cake.

Set oven to 350°F or Mark 4. In a bowl, rub the fat into the flour until the mixture resembles fine breadcrumbs. Then stir in the spices, sugar, fruit, peel and ground almonds and combine well. Break the eggs into a bowl, combine very lightly with a fork – do not beat – and then stir into the mixture, adding a little milk, if necessary, to produce a *very* stiff dough. Grease a baking sheet and dust with flour. On a lightly floured surface, form the dough into a round and place on the baking sheet. Brush the top with milk to glaze. Bake for about 50 to 60 minutes, or until a skewer inserted into the cake comes out clean. Cool on a wire rack. As Bury Simnel Cake is not confined to a tin, the dough *must* be stiff enough to hold its shape during cooking, but be prepared for it to 'spread' a little.

Wet Nelly

½ lb. fresh white breadcrumbs
5 fl. oz. milk or water
2 teaspoons mixed spice
Grated rind of ½ a lemon or orange (optional)
4 oz. finely chopped suet
4 oz. soft brown sugar
A 'walnut' of butter
A little extra brown sugar

Soak the breadcrumbs in the milk or water for 30 minutes. Well grease an 8 inch square roasting tin. Set oven to 350°F or Mark 4. Stir in the mixed spice, lemon or orange rind (if desired), suet and brown sugar and combine well together. Turn into the tin and smooth the surface. Dot with butter and sprinkle over the extra sugar. Bake for 1 to 1½ hours until firm and golden. Cut into slices and serve hot or cold.

A Northern version of Bread Pudding, originally made with crusts left over from bread sauce.

Chipping below the Forest of Bowland

Everton Toffee

1 lb. demerara sugar
A 'scant' ½ pint water
8 oz. unsalted butter
4 level tablespoons golden syrup
A few drops of oil of lemon (optional)

First made in the 18th century, by a young cook named Molly Bushell, this toffee is traditionally eaten on 5th November.

Well oil a square 8 to 10 inch baking tin. Put the sugar and water into a heavy-based saucepan over a low heat and stir until all the sugar has dissolved. Stir in the butter and syrup and continue cooking, until the mixture has turned a rich golden brown and has reached the 'soft crack' stage (270–280°F). Check the temperature with great care, using a sugar thermometer. If a sugar thermometer is not available, drop a little of the mixture into cold water. When it separates into hard threads it has reached the 'soft-crack' stage. Remove from the heat and stir in the oil of lemon (if desired). Pour into the tin and leave to cool and mark into squares; or break into pieces when cold.

Spiced Yule Bread

1 lb. flour
Pinch of salt
2 teaspoons mixed spice
1 teaspoon finely grated orange or lemon rind
2 oz. butter
2 oz. lard
4 oz. sugar
4 oz. currants or sultanas
4 oz. raisins
1 tablespoon candied peel, finely chopped
1 egg, beaten
¾ oz. fresh yeast
1 teaspoon sugar
Warm milk

Traditionally served at Christmas, with Lancashire cheese and mulled ale.

Sift together the flour, salt and mixed spice and stir in the orange or lemon rind. Rub in the butter and lard until the mixture resembles fine breadcrumbs, then stir in 4 oz. sugar, and the fruit and peel. Add the beaten egg and stir lightly. Cream the yeast and teaspoon of sugar together and add a little warm milk. When frothy, add to the flour mixture with sufficient warm milk to make a soft, but not sticky, dough. Cover and leave to rise until doubled in bulk. Turn out on to a lightly floured surface and knead gently for 1 to 2 minutes. Shape and put into a well-greased 2 lb. loaf tin and prove for a further 10 to 15 minutes. Set oven to 400°F or Mark 6. Bake for 50 minutes to 1 hour or until golden brown and well risen. Remove and, whilst hot, brush the top with a little warm sugar water to give a sheen. Turn out and cool on a wire rack. Serve sliced, with or without butter.

Lord Street, Southport

Lancashire Sly Cake

2 tablespoons dark rum
8 oz. currants
12 oz. shortcrust pastry (ideally made with butter)
2 tablespoons soft brown sugar
½ teaspoon ground nutmeg
A 'walnut' of butter
Milk or beaten egg to glaze

Sprinkle the rum over the currants in a bowl and allow to stand for 30 minutes. Set oven to 400°F or Mark 6. Roll out the pastry on a lightly floured surface and divide in half. Roll each half into a circle approximately 7 inches in diameter. Place one circle on a well-greased baking sheet and turn up the edge slightly to form a rim. Spread the rum-soaked currants on the pastry. Mix together the sugar and nutmeg and sprinkle over the currants, then dot with butter. Cover with the other half of the pastry, dampen and seal the edges very well and trim neatly. Brush with milk or beaten egg to glaze and bake for 30 minutes or until golden brown. Serve hot with custard or cream, or cold in slices. Serves 4 to 6.

It is also traditional to make Sly Cakes in a square shape as well as round. If preferred, the Sly Cake can be made in a greased 7-inch shallow pie plate.

Potato Scones

1 lb. 'floury' potatoes, peeled and cut into pieces
1 teaspoon salt
1½ oz. butter or margarine
About 4 to 4½ oz. flour

Cook the potatoes in boiling, salted water until tender. Drain well, then mash until smooth. While the potatoes are still hot, add the salt and the butter or margarine, then stir in sufficient flour to make a stiff dough. Turn out on to a lightly floured surface, knead lightly, then roll out to about ¼-inch thickness. Cut into 2 inch rounds. Grease a griddle or heavy based frying pan and cook the scones for about 4 minutes on each side, or until golden brown. Serve hot with butter and Lancashire cheese. Makes about 12.

Potato Scones were often made with left-over mashed potato, in which case, the potato has to be heated through in the oven before being used.

Stuffed Hearts or Love in Disguise

4 lambs' hearts

STUFFING:
2 oz. butter
1 onion, peeled and chopped
2 oz. breadcrumbs
1 dessertspoon fresh sage, finely chopped
Grated rind of ½ a lemon
Pinch of nutmeg
Salt and black pepper
1 egg yolk
1 to 2 tablespoons seasoned flour
¾ pint lamb stock
Fresh sage leaves to garnish

Set oven to 300°F or Mark 2. Wash and trim the hearts. Stuffing: Melt half the butter in a pan and fry the onion lightly. In a bowl, mix together the breadcrumbs, sage, lemon rind and nutmeg, then add the onion. Season, then bind the mixture with the egg yolk. Stuff the hearts and, if necessary, sew up with fine kitchen string to contain the stuffing. Dust with seasoned flour. Melt the remaining butter in a frying pan and brown the hearts lightly on all sides. Place in an ovenproof casserole, pour on the stock, cover and cook for 2 hours or until tender. Remove the string (if used) and serve the hearts garnished with sage leaves and accompanied by mashed potatoes and red cabbage. Strain the stock and serve separately. Serves 4.

Martinmas Beef

3 lb. brisket of beef
½ onion, peeled and sliced
A 1-inch piece of root ginger, finely chopped
3 blades mace
½ teaspoon ground nutmeg
¼ teaspoon ground cloves
Salt
½ pint white wine
2 tablespoons white wine vinegar
1 oz. cornflour, mixed to smooth paste with a little water

Set oven to 275°F or Mark 1. Place the beef in an ovenproof casserole, with the onion, spices and salt. Mix the wine and vinegar together and pour over. Cover and cook for 3 to 3½ hours. Remove the beef and place on a warm plate. Strain the liquid into a saucepan, add the cornflour, bring to the boil stirring continually until thickened. Serve the beef with carrots and mashed potatoes, with the sauce served separately. Serves 4 to 6.

St. Martin's Day, 11th November was, by tradition, a time of celebration in the farming community.

St. Michael's on Wyre

Rhubarb Tart

8 oz. shortcrust pastry
¾ to1 lb. rhubarb, wiped and trimmed
2 teaspoons orange or lemon juice
3 to 4 oz. sugar
½ teaspoon of cinnamon
½ oz. butter
Milk or beaten egg to glaze

If desired, any pastry trimmings may be cut into neat strips, twisted like barley sugar and used to make a lattice pattern on the tart. Dampen the ends of the strips and press, in a criss-cross pattern, to the edge of the tart to secure them in position, then brush with milk or beaten egg to glaze, before baking.

Set oven to 400°F or Mark 6. Roll out the pastry on a lightly floured surface and use to line a greased 7 inch flan dish, trimming the edges neatly. Cover with foil and bake blind for 10 minutes. Cut the rhubarb into neat, even pieces and place in a saucepan with a little water to which the orange or lemon juice has been added. Cook the rhubarb until the pieces are soft, but still hold their shape. Drain well. Remove the flan from the oven and sprinkle half the sugar over the base. Mix the remaining sugar with the cinnamon. Arrange the rhubarb pieces in a neat circular pattern in the flan, then sprinkle over them the remaining sugar and dot with butter, Brush with milk or beaten egg to glaze and bake for 30 to 40 minutes or until the pastry is golden brown. Serve hot or cold with custard or cream. Serves 4.

Bakestone Cake

½ oz. butter
12 oz. apples, peeled, cored and sliced
1 to 2 oz. brown sugar
Pinch of ground nutmeg or cinnamon
8 oz. shortcrust pastry

This is more of a pudding than a cake, and was originally cooked on a 'bakestone', a flat stone heated through for cooking bread and scones.

Melt the butter in a saucepan, then add the apples, sugar and spice. Cook gently to soften the apples, but do not allow them to become pulpy. Roll out the pastry on a lightly floured surface and divide in half. Form each half into a circle about 7 inches in diameter. Place the fruit in the centre of one circle, leaving about ¾ inch clear round the edge. Moisten the edge with milk and top with the remaining circle, sealing the edges well and trimming neatly. Brush a griddle or large, heavy-based frying pan with lard. Heat thoroughly, then, using two fish slices, place the cake on the griddle or in the frying pan. Cook on one side for 10 to 12 minutes, then turn and cook on the other, until both sides are golden brown. Remove with the fish slices. Serve hot, sprinkled with sugar and accompanied by custard or cream. Serves 4 to 6.

Beside the Leeds and Liverpool Canal at Rufford

Fig Pudding

8 oz. dried figs
2 oz. raisins
3 oz. butter
3 oz. soft brown sugar
3 oz. flour
2 oz. fresh white breadcrumbs
1 oz. ground almonds
Pinch of mixed spice
Grated rind of ½ a lemon
1 egg
2 to 3 tablespoons brandy, rum, Madeira or sherry

Another dish traditionally served on Mothering Sunday, figs being a symbol of fruitfulness.

Soak the figs and raisins overnight in cold weak tea, to which a little lemon juice has been added. Next morning, drain the fruit well and chop the figs finely. In a bowl, cream the butter and sugar together, then fold in the flour a little at a time. Add the breadcrumbs, ground almonds, spice, lemon rind, figs and raisins and combine well. Beat the egg with the brandy, rum, Madeira or sherry and add to the mixture. Stir well, then turn into a 1½ to 2 pint buttered pudding basin. Cover with buttered grease-proof paper and a pudding cloth tied with string or with kitchen foil. Place in a steamer over a saucepan of boiling water. Cover and steam for 3½ to 4 hours, topping up the water as necessary, until the pudding is springy and well risen. Turn out on to a warm plate and serve with custard or cream. Serves 4 to 6.

Oatmeal Bread

8 oz. medium oatmeal
½ pint milk
2 fl. oz. warm water
1 teaspoon castor sugar
3 teaspoons dried yeast
12 oz. strong white flour
1 dessertspoon salt
2 tablespoons melted butter
A little extra oatmeal

Put oatmeal and milk in a bowl, mix and soak for 30 minutes. Dissolve sugar in warm water, then stir in yeast. Leave in warm place for about 10 minutes until dissolved and frothy. In a warmed bowl mix together soaked oatmeal, flour, salt and melted butter, add yeast and mix until a 'scone-like' dough is formed. Turn dough on to lightly floured surface and knead for about 10 minutes, until smooth and pliable. Shape into a ball, cover and leave to rise until doubled in bulk. Knock back and knead for further 2 to 3 minutes, until dough is firm. Shape into two round 'cobs', place on lightly floured baking sheet, cover and prove again until doubled in bulk. Set oven to 450°F or Mark 8. Brush tops with milk and sprinkle on a little extra oatmeal. Bake in centre of oven for about 25 minutes. Cool on a wire rack.

Spare Rib Pie

8 oz. shortcrust pastry
1½ to 2 lb. pork spare ribs
A little seasoned flour
A little cooking oil or dripping
Salt and black pepper
1 tablespoon chopped fresh parsley
½ pint beef or pork stock, thickened with a little cornflour
Milk or beaten egg to glaze

Set oven to 350°F or Mark 4. Remove the meat from the bones and cut into pieces. Dust with seasoned flour. Heat the oil or dripping in a frying pan and brown the meat lightly. Drain well and place in a 1 to 2 pint pie dish. Season and sprinkle with the parsley and then pour on the stock. Roll out the pastry on a lightly floured surface and cover the pie, sealing the edges and trimming neatly; use the trimmings to decorate. Make a small steam hole. Brush with milk or beaten egg to glaze. Bake for 40 to 50 minutes until the pastry is golden brown. Serve cold accompanied by pickled beetroot. Serves 4 to 6.

METRIC CONVERSIONS

The weights, measures and oven temperatures used in the preceding recipes can be easily converted to their metric equivalents.

Weights

Avoirdupois	Metric
1 oz.	just under 30 grams
4 oz. (¼ lb.)	app. 115 grams
8 oz. (½ lb.)	app. 230 grams
1 lb.	454 grams

Liquid Measures

Imperial	Metric
1 tablespoon (liquid only)	20 millilitres
1 fl. oz.	app. 30 millilitres
1 gill (¼ pt.)	app. 145 millilitres
½ pt.	app. 285 millilitres
1 pt.	app. 570 millilitres
1 qt.	app. 1.140 litres

Oven Temperatures

	°Fahrenheit	Gas Mark	°Celsius
Slow	300	2	140
	325	3	158
Moderate	350	4	177
	375	5	190
	400	6	204
Hot	425	7	214
	450	8	232
	500	9	260

Flour as specified in these recipes refers to Plain Flour unless otherwise described